Top 50 Quick Facts About the Human Body

Science Book Age 6
Children's Science Education Books

BABY PROFESSOR

EDUCATION KIDS

You know your own body better than anybody else does. You're the first one to know when you get a cold or stub a toe! But there's a lot of interesting stuff you may not know about your own body, or anybody else's. Read on and learn fifty things you may not have known before about our wonderful bodies.

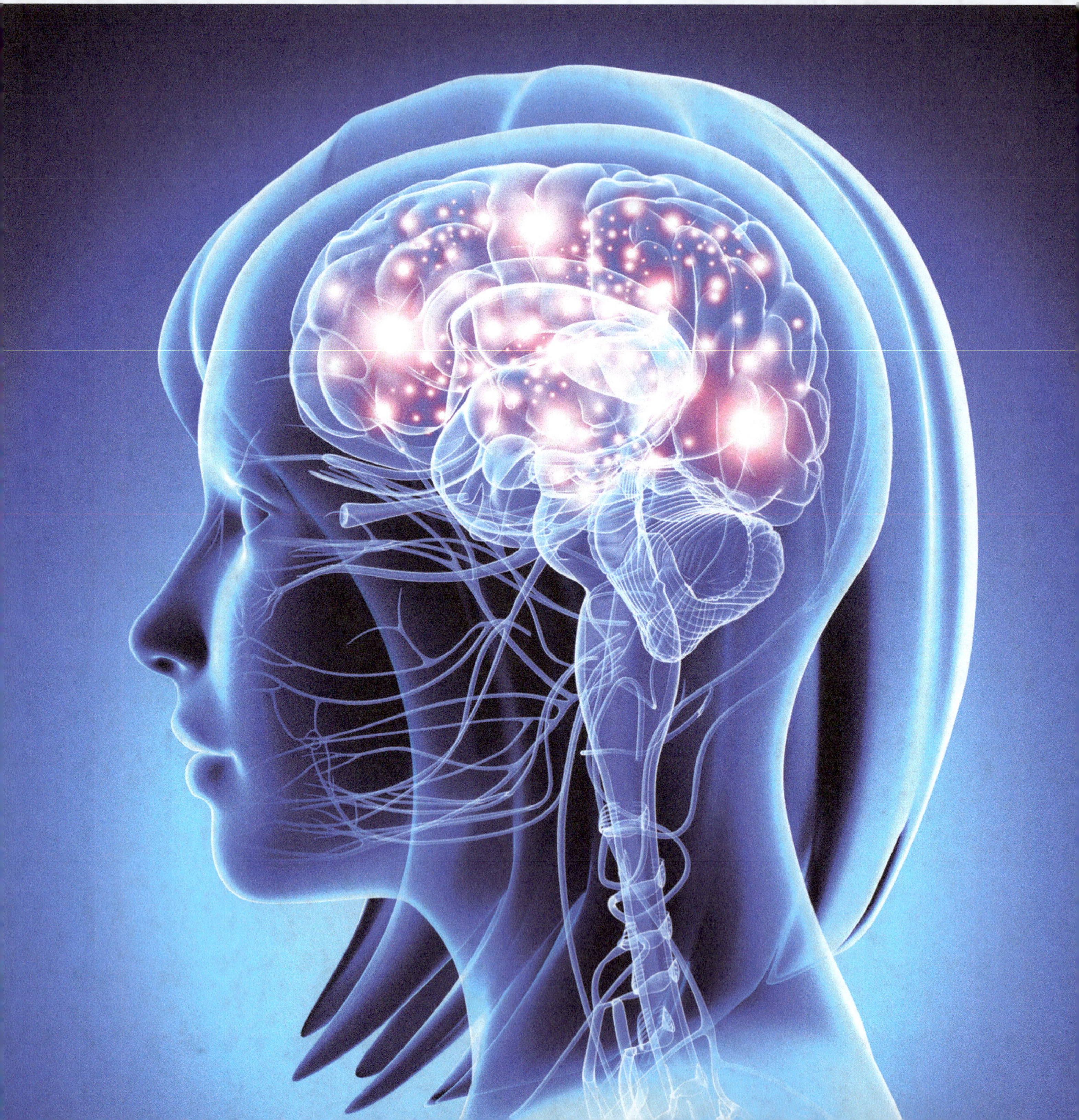

1. Your brain sends and gets messages at speeds up to 170 miles an hour. This is how come you can pull your hand away from something hot without even deciding to do it. Your brain got the news and made the decision for you while you were still getting ready to say, "Ow!"

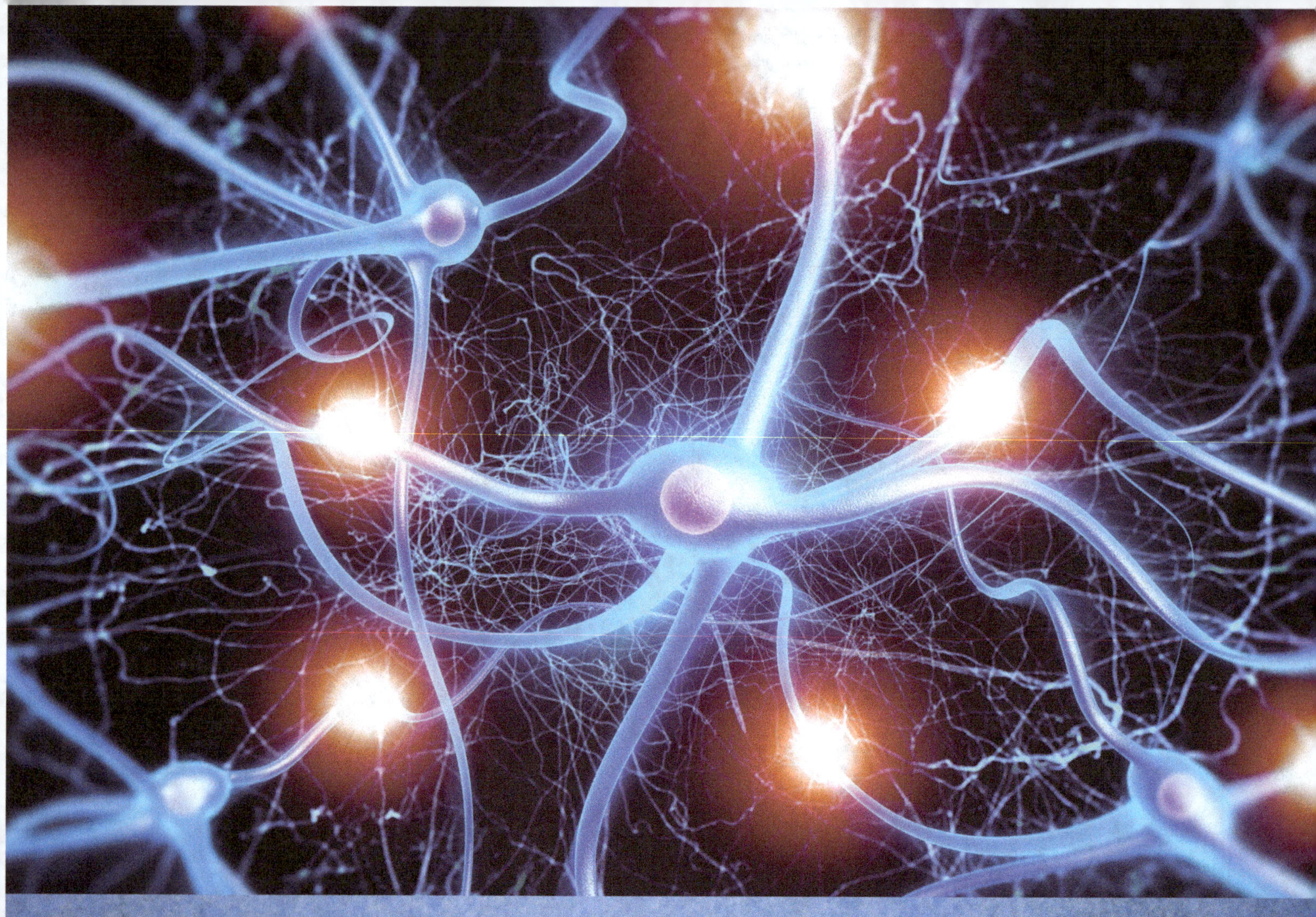

2. One brain cell can hold five times as much information as you can find in an encyclopedia, with room to spare.

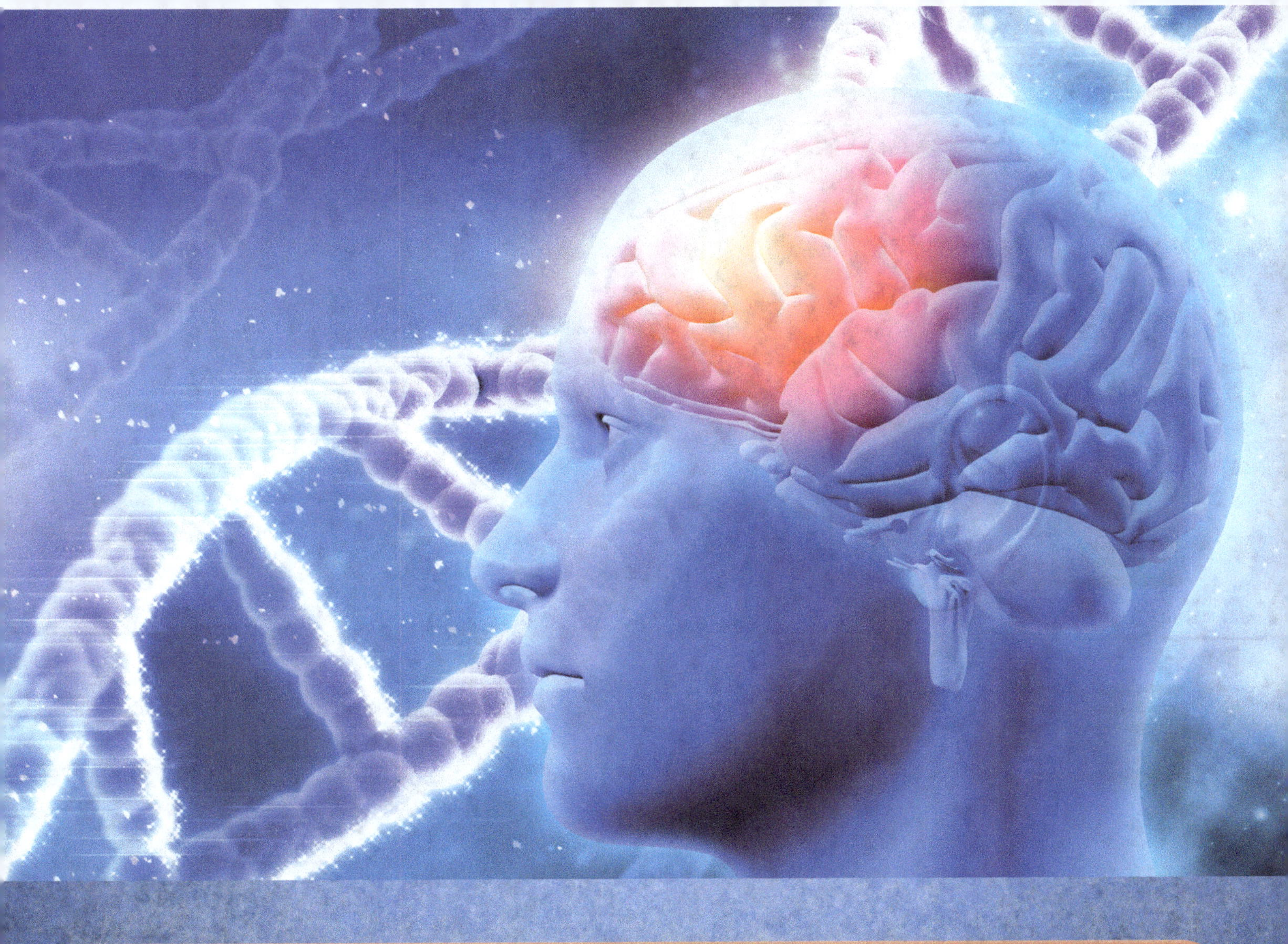

3. Your brain makes up about 2% of the mass of your body, but uses 20% of the oxygen you take in.

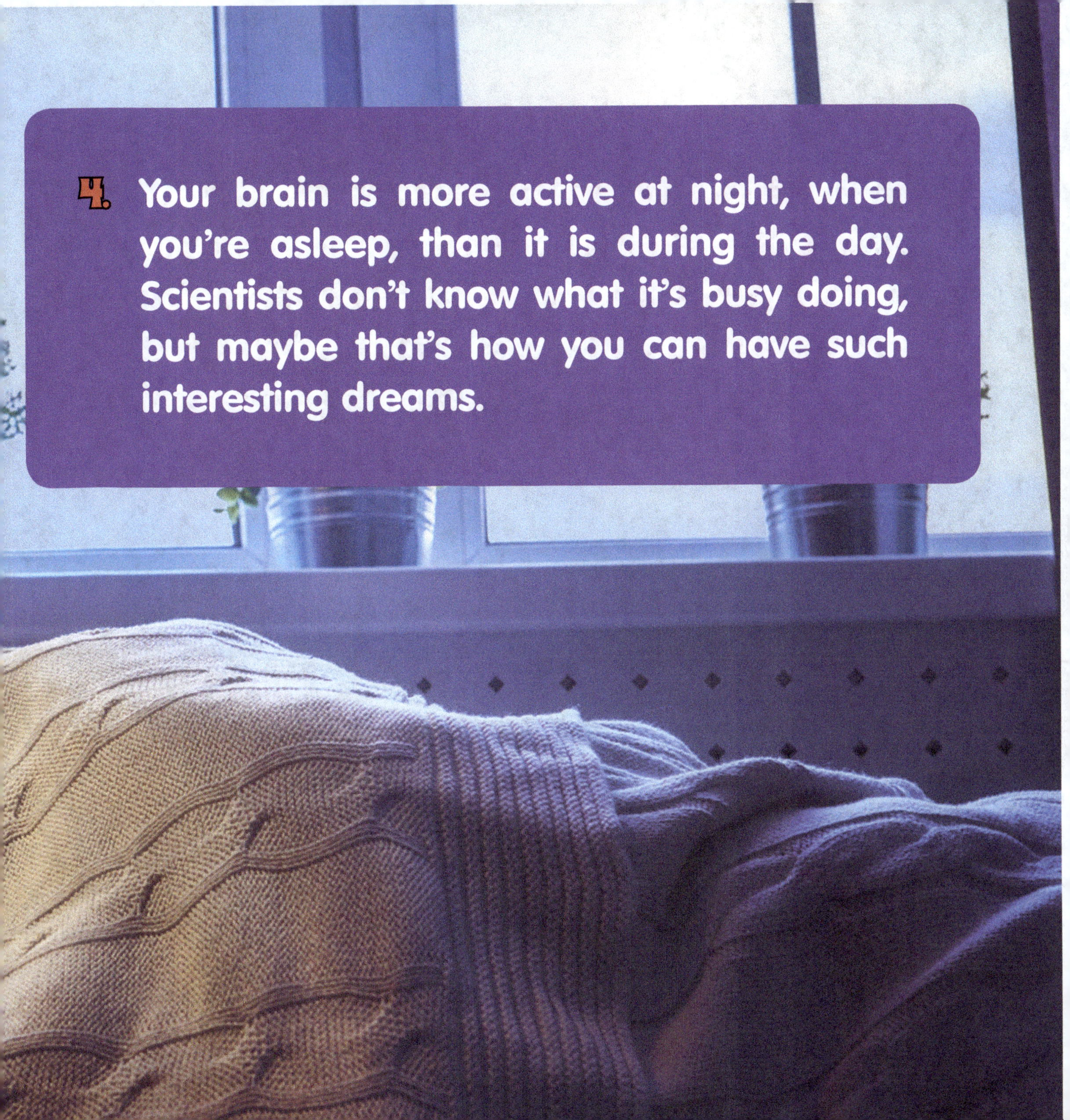

4. Your brain is more active at night, when you're asleep, than it is during the day. Scientists don't know what it's busy doing, but maybe that's how you can have such interesting dreams.

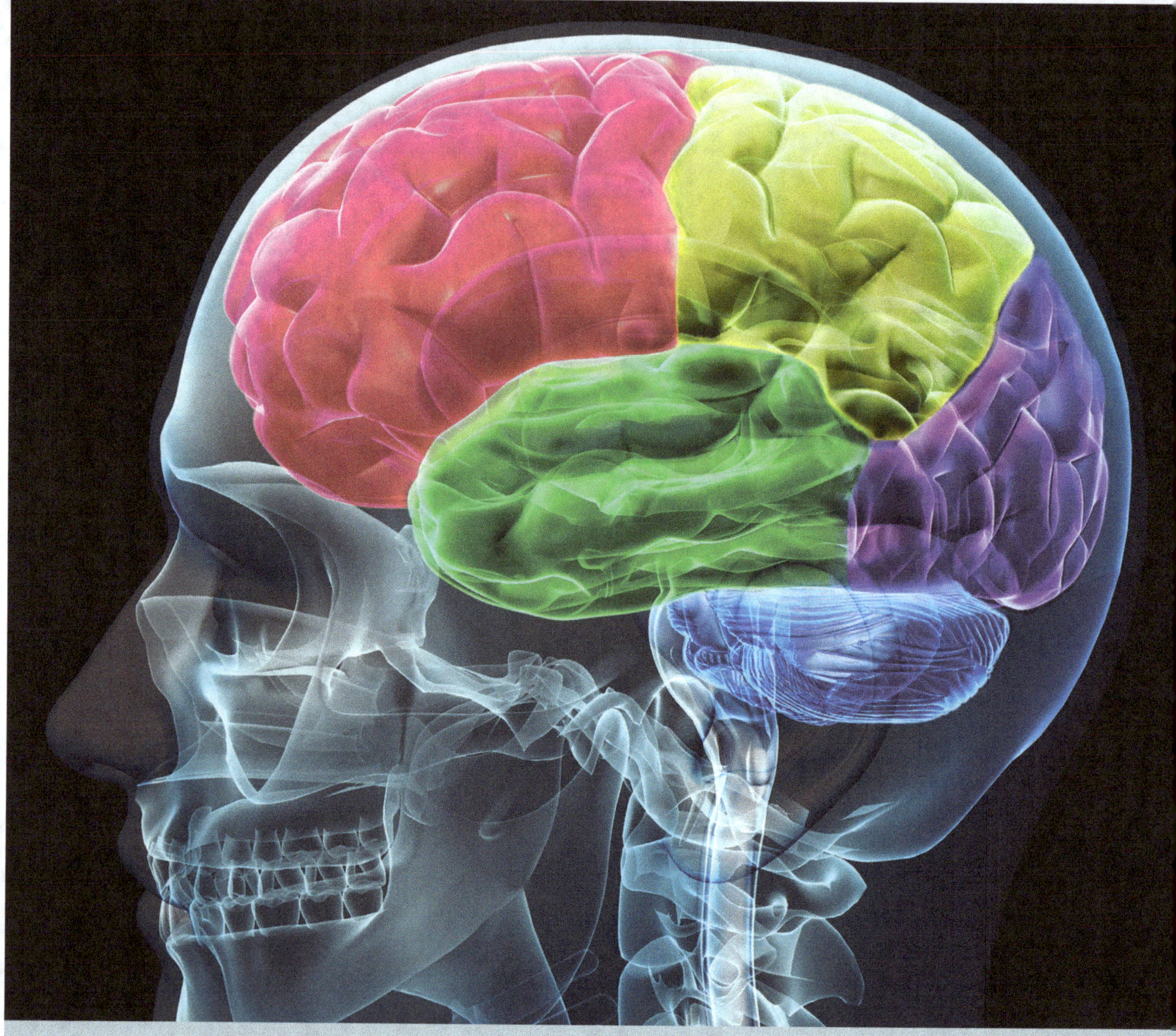

Colored sections of a Human Brain

5. Your brain itself doesn't feel any pain. There are no sensory nerves inside the brain itself, although there are plenty on your head. When you feel pain, it's some other part of your body reporting that pain to your brain.

6. Your brain is 80% water. It's not solid like a book or a pillow. That's why drinking lots of water to keep the brain well supplied can help you think more clearly.

1. Your heart beats so strongly it could shoot blood 30 feet. It has to push hard to get the blood to every single part of your body.

2. Your stomach acids could dissolve metal. Your stomach and intestines have special linings to protect them from the powerful acids, which your body uses to break down food you eat so you can use its nutrients. But please don't start eating metal!

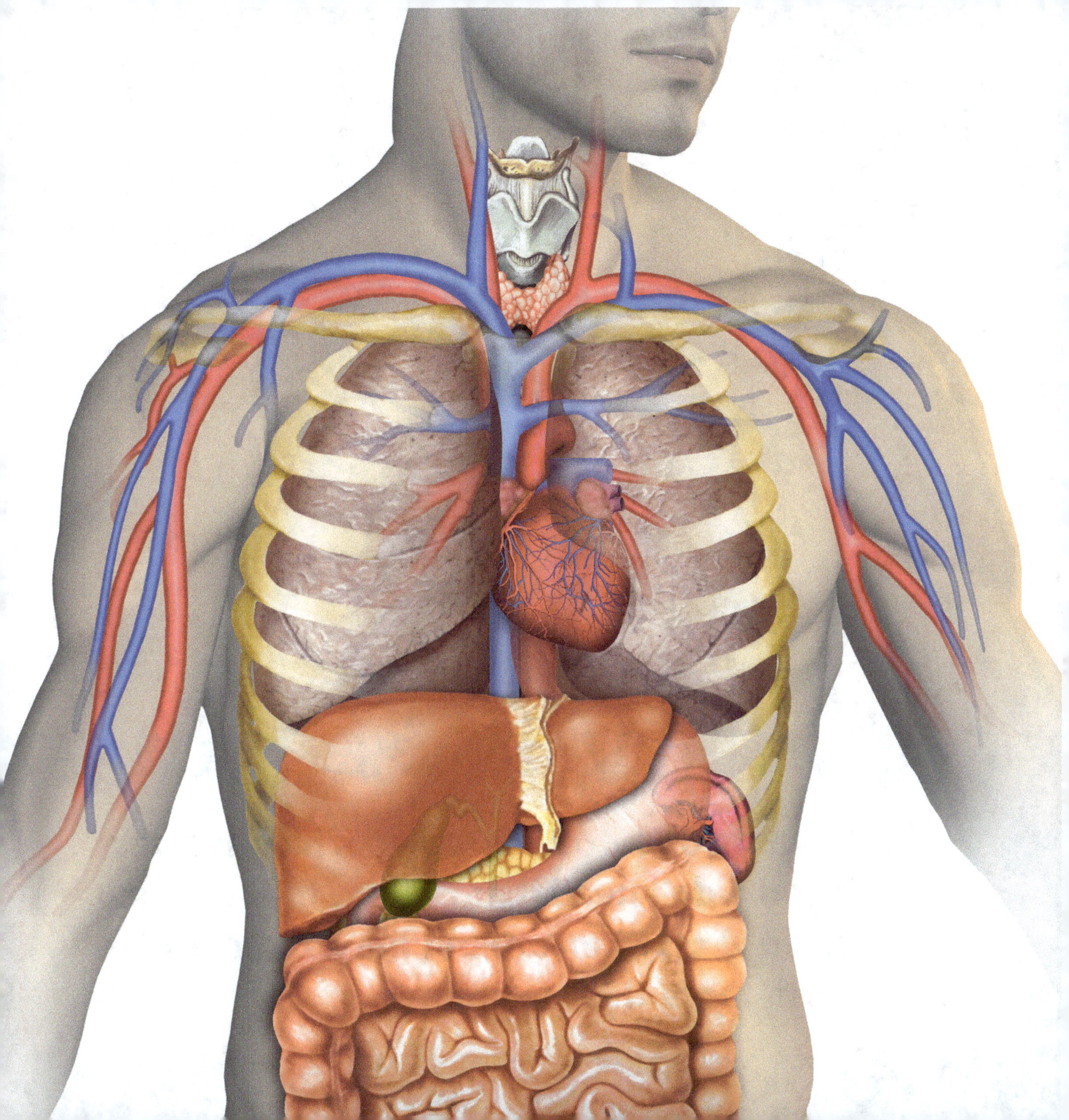

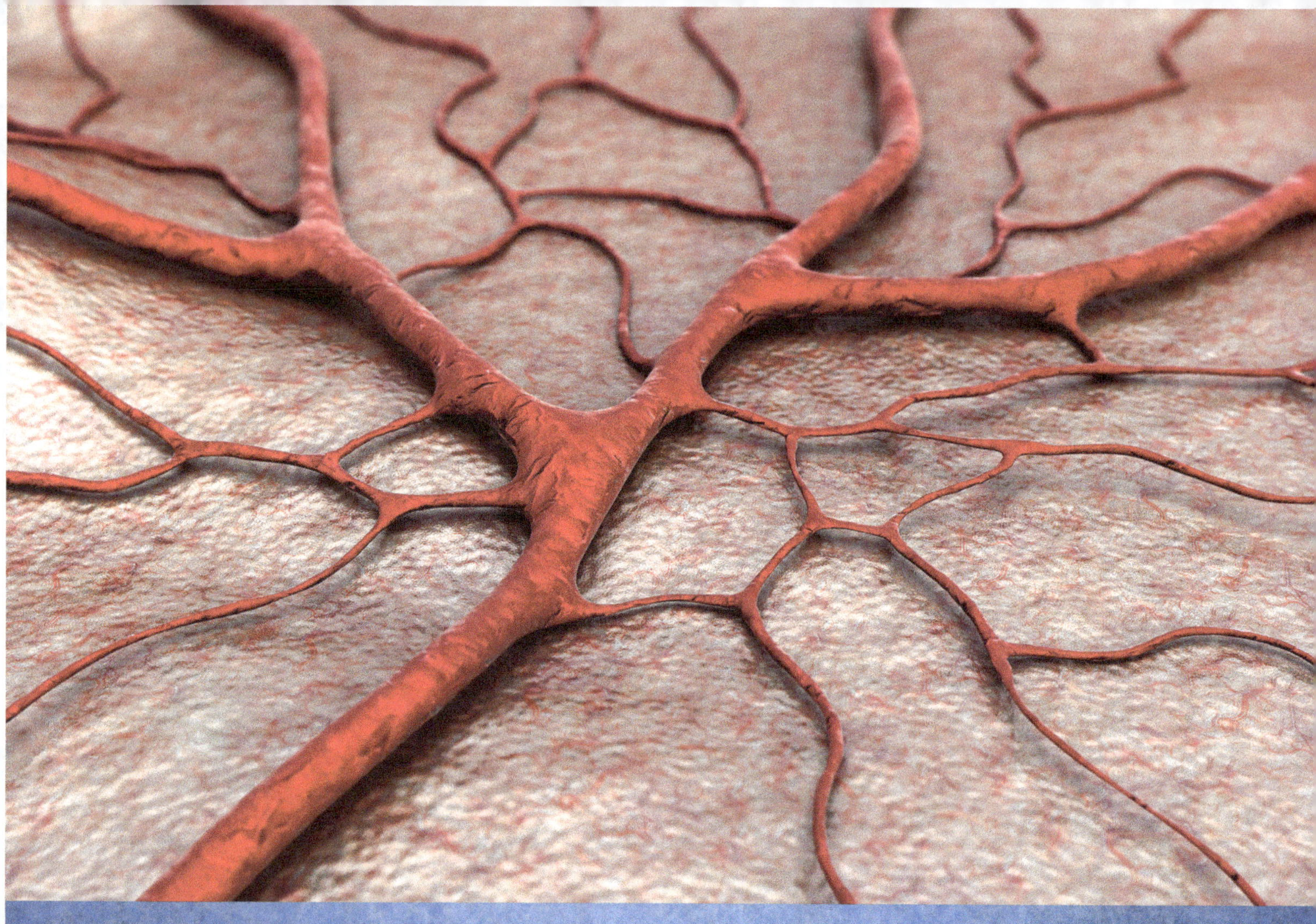

3. You have about 60,000 miles of blood vessels. If you didn't need them where they are, you could wrap them around the equator of the Earth more than two times.

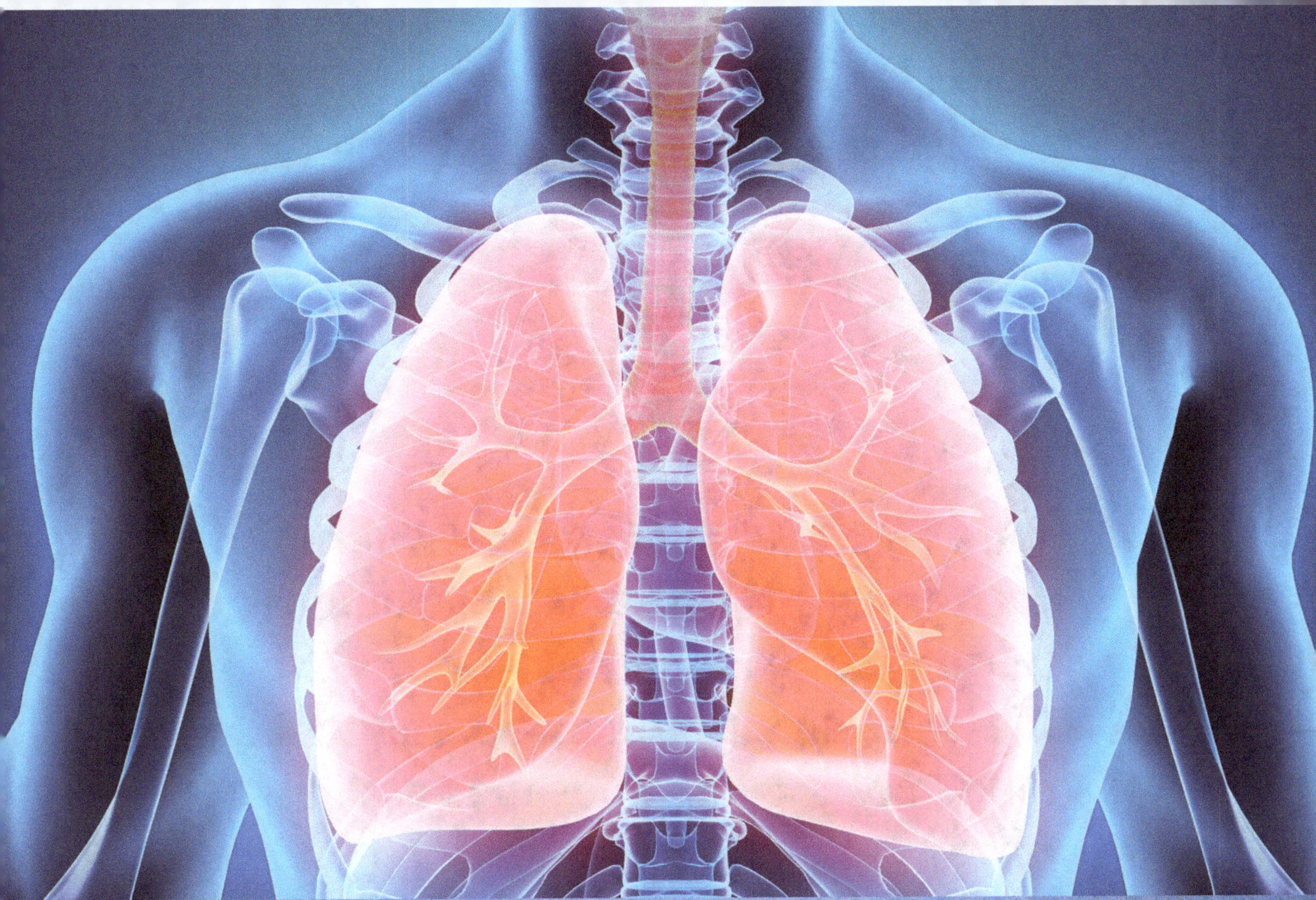

4. You have two lungs. The left one is smaller than the right one so there is room in your chest for your heart. Your heart is almost in the center of your chest, but it leans to the left to take advantage of the space your left lung provides.

5. You could lose a lot of most internal organs and still survive. It wouldn't be fun, but you could live an active life with only one kidney, only one lung, most of your intestines and just one quarter of your liver.

Sense of smell

1. After you over-eat at a meal, you can't hear as well. So eat less before you go to the concert!

2. Only about a third of people have "20-20" vision, which is what is considered normal. Everyone else, if they're not blind, is nearsighted or farsighted.

3. For you to taste something in your mouth, your saliva has to dissolve some of it. If it can't dissolve it, you can't taste it.

4. Women, in general, have a much better sense of smell than men. They are much better at identifying citrus, vanilla, coffee and cinnamon.

5. Unfortunately, about 2% of people have no sense of smell at all.

6. Your nose can identify up to 50,000 different smells.

7. The sense of smell is more closely connected to your memory of events than any other sense.

8. Any noise makes your eyes dilate a little. It's like a little visual flinch.

9. Everybody has a unique smell, except for twins, who smell like each other. Newborns recognize their mothers by their smell.

A happy little girl smelling a flower.

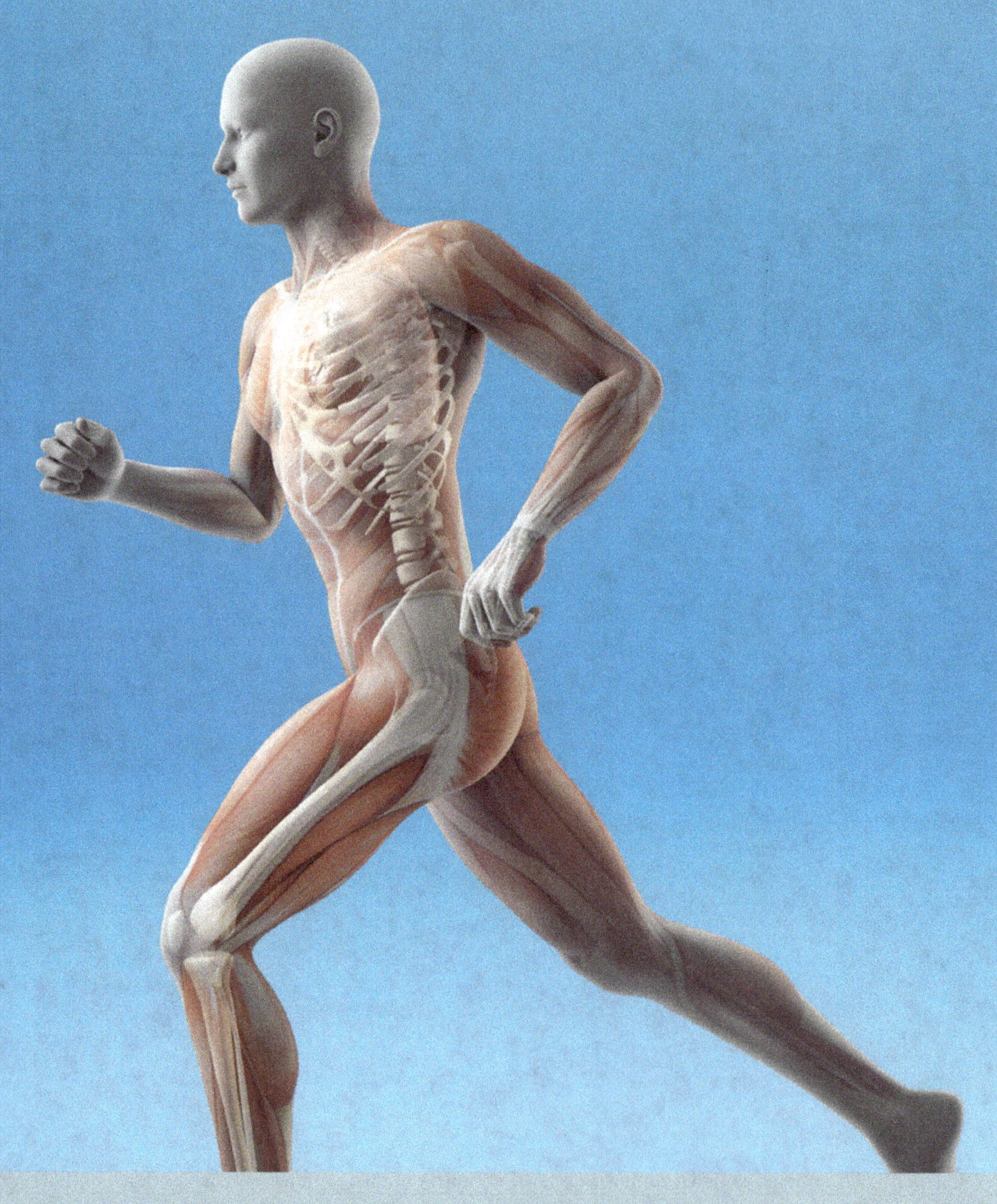

Running muscle anatomy of a man

MUSCLES AND BONES

1. It takes 17 muscles to smile and 43 to frown.

2. People are born with over 300 bones, but by the time they are grown up, many small bones have fused together and your bone-count is down to about 206.

3. We're taller after a night's sleep. While we lie down the cartilage between our bones has a chance to expand. A day of standing and walking squeezes them a bit flatter.

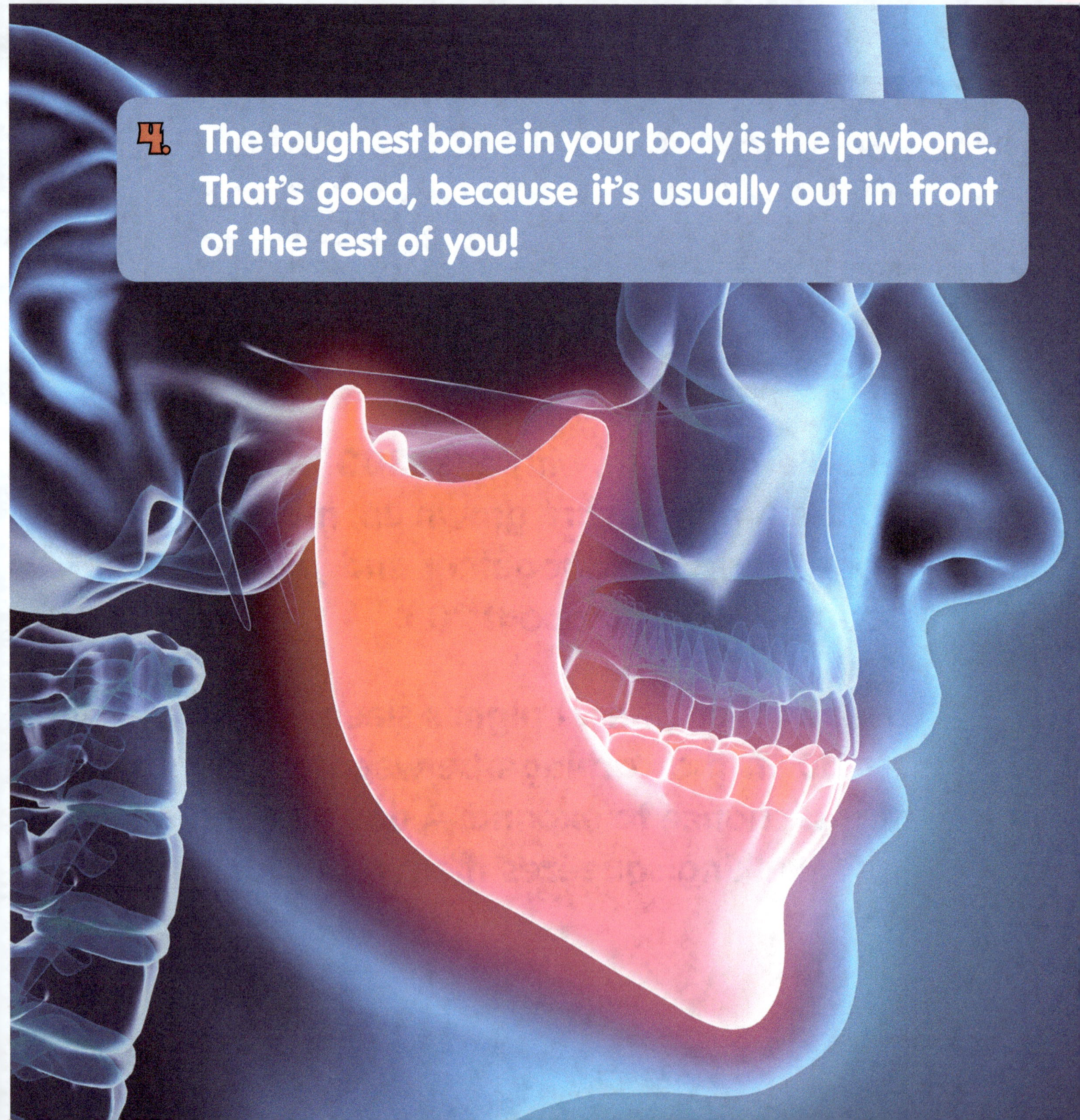
4. The toughest bone in your body is the jawbone. That's good, because it's usually out in front of the rest of you!

5. You use around 200 muscles to take a single step, and most of us take about 10,000 steps each day.

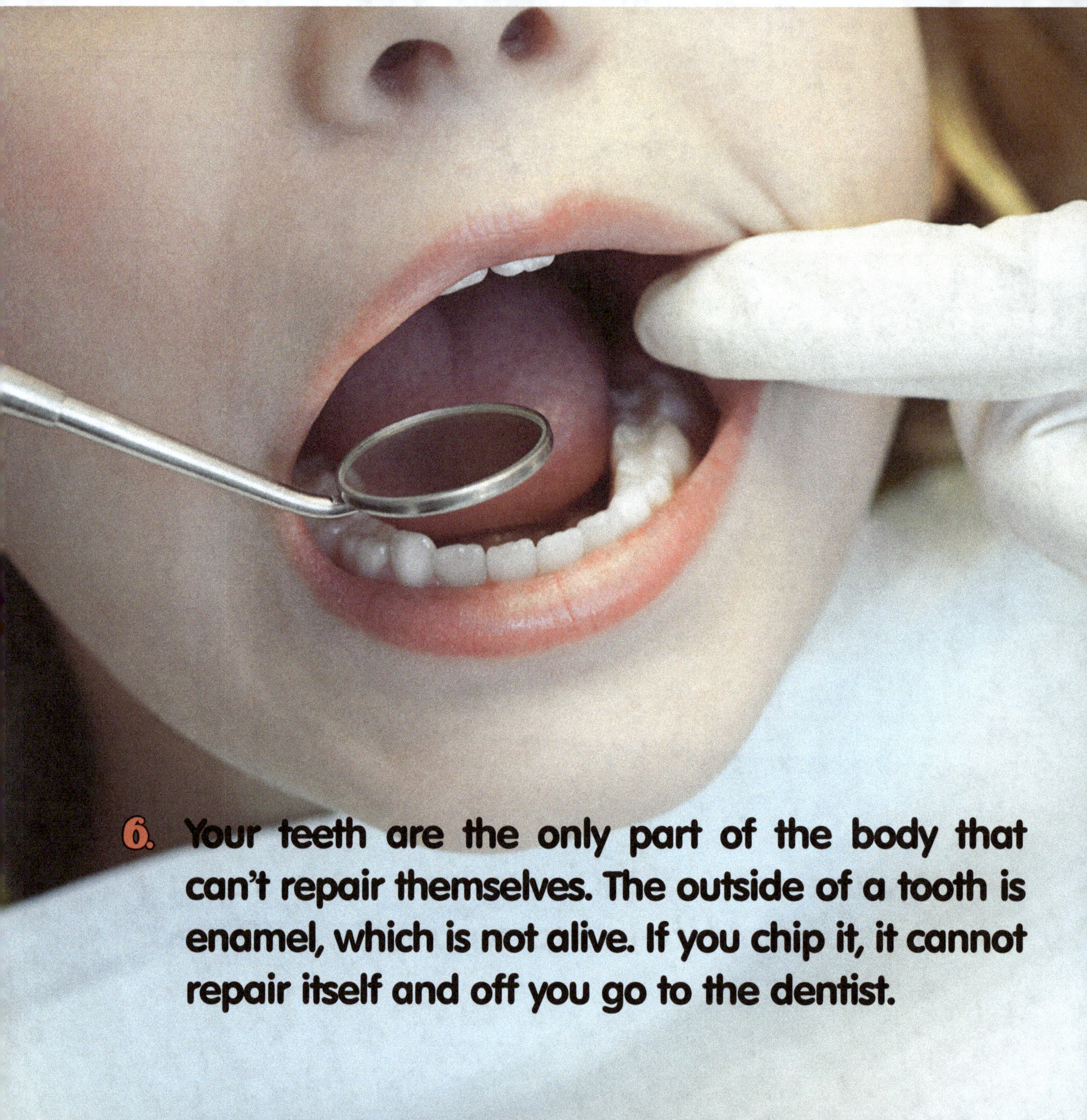

6. Your teeth are the only part of the body that can't repair themselves. The outside of a tooth is enamel, which is not alive. If you chip it, it cannot repair itself and off you go to the dentist.

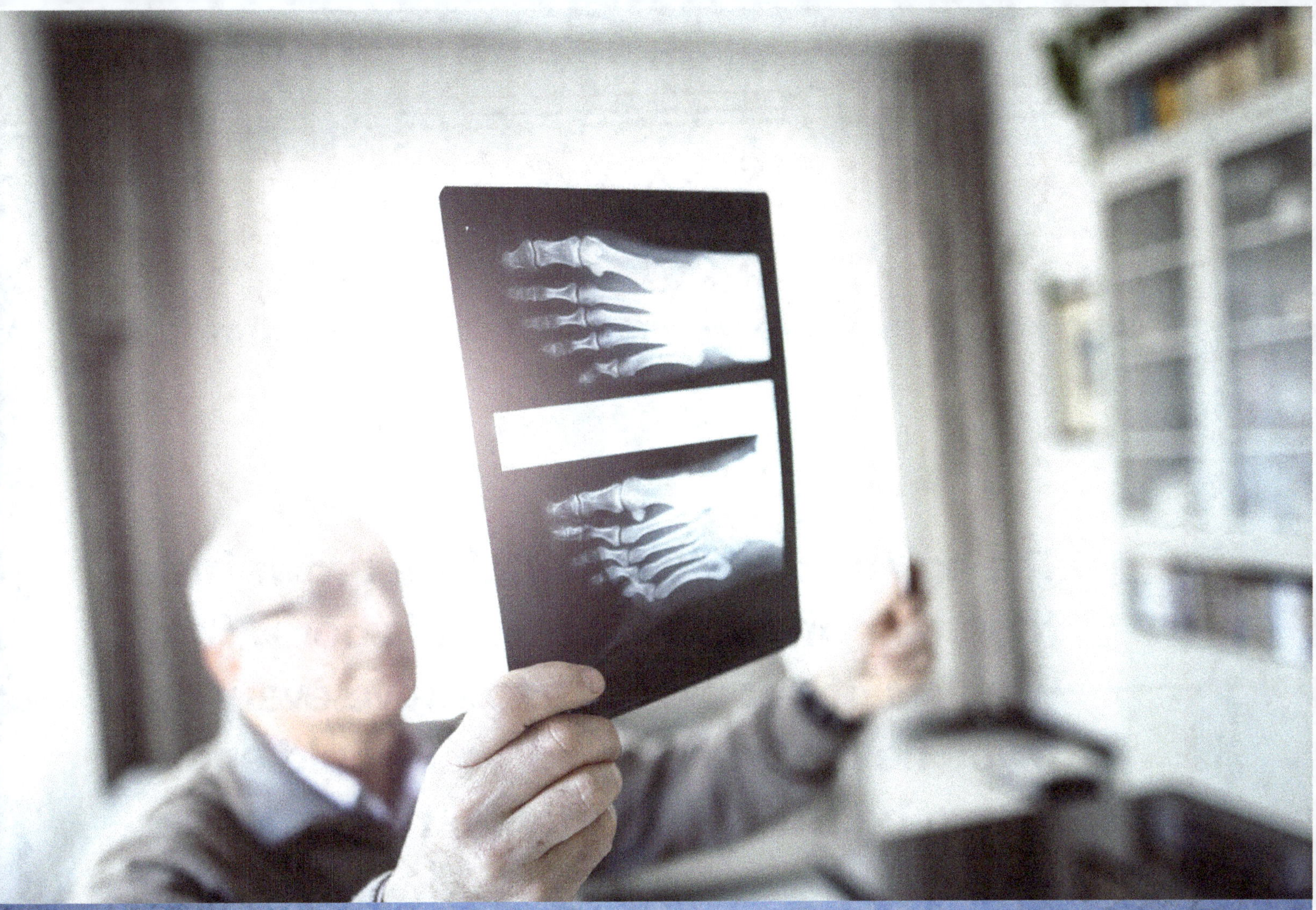

7. One quarter of the bones in your body are in your two feet—that's over fifty out of about 200.

HAIR AND NAILS

1. The hair on an adult man's face grows faster than hair anywhere else on his body. That's why lots of people have to shave every day. If you never, ever shaved, you would end up with a beard up to thirty feet long.

Man and woman's hair

2. A strand of hair from a man's head is twice as thick as a strand from a woman's head.

3. The nails on your longest fingers grow faster than the nails on your shorter fingers. And the nail on the longest finger of your dominant hand grows fastest of all. Nobody has figured out why.

4. Blonde people have the most hair follicles, around 150,000, on their heads. Redheads have the fewest, around 85,000.

5. Fingernails grow about four times faster than toenails.

6. It's really hard to destroy hair. Hair can resist almost any treatment except burning, including many strong chemicals.

Baby Teeth Coming In

1. Your teeth start growing about six months before you're born.

2. By the time a fetus has been developing for three months, it has a full set of fingerprints. Each person's fingerprints are unique, and they don't change through your whole life.

3. Although you inherit your eye color from your parents, all babies enter the world with blue eyes. The melanin pignment in babies' eyes has to get used to being out of the womb and in the world before it knows how dark to get, and you can see the true color of the baby's eyes.

4. We think of babies as weak and helpless, but if they were as big as an ox, they would be stronger than the ox. Their muscles may be small, but they are powerful!

5. You were once nothing more than a single cell. When the mother's egg and the father's sperm combine, they are a single cell for about an hour. After that, the process of cell division begins and the fetus starts its nine-month development.

YOUR BODY AT WORK

1. When you sneeze, you project droplets at about 100 mph. Please cover your mouth and nose!

2. When you cough, and don't cover your mouth, you are spraying stuff out at 60 mph.

3. People blink about 13 times a minute, but by the end of a day a woman will have blinked about twice as often as a man has.

4. When your bladder is full it's not surprising you need to go pee. Your bladder at that point is about the size of a softball.

5. Over your whole life, you produce enough saliva to fill two large swimming pools.

6. The average person farts about 14 times a day. Most of the time nobody, not even the person, notices the event.

Man farting

7. Your eyes stay the same size for your whole life, but your nose and ears keep growing.

8. Your feet have over 300,000 sweat glands and can create over a pint of sweat each day. That's why your gym shoes can get smelly!

INJURY AND ILLNESS

1. More people die of heart attacks on Mondays than on any other day of the week. It may be a combination of too much fun over the weekend and the stress of going back to work.

2. Your sleep is more important than your food. If you have enough water, you could survive and function for as much as a month or even more without food. However, if you go without sleep for just a few days, your personality changes, you begin to hallucinate, you have trouble forming words, and you may not be able to perform simple actions like opening a lock.

Stressed mom

3. Being under stress when you are sick can make your illness much worse. That's one reason people advise you to take a break, go to bed, and forget about your work or duties when you feel under the weather.

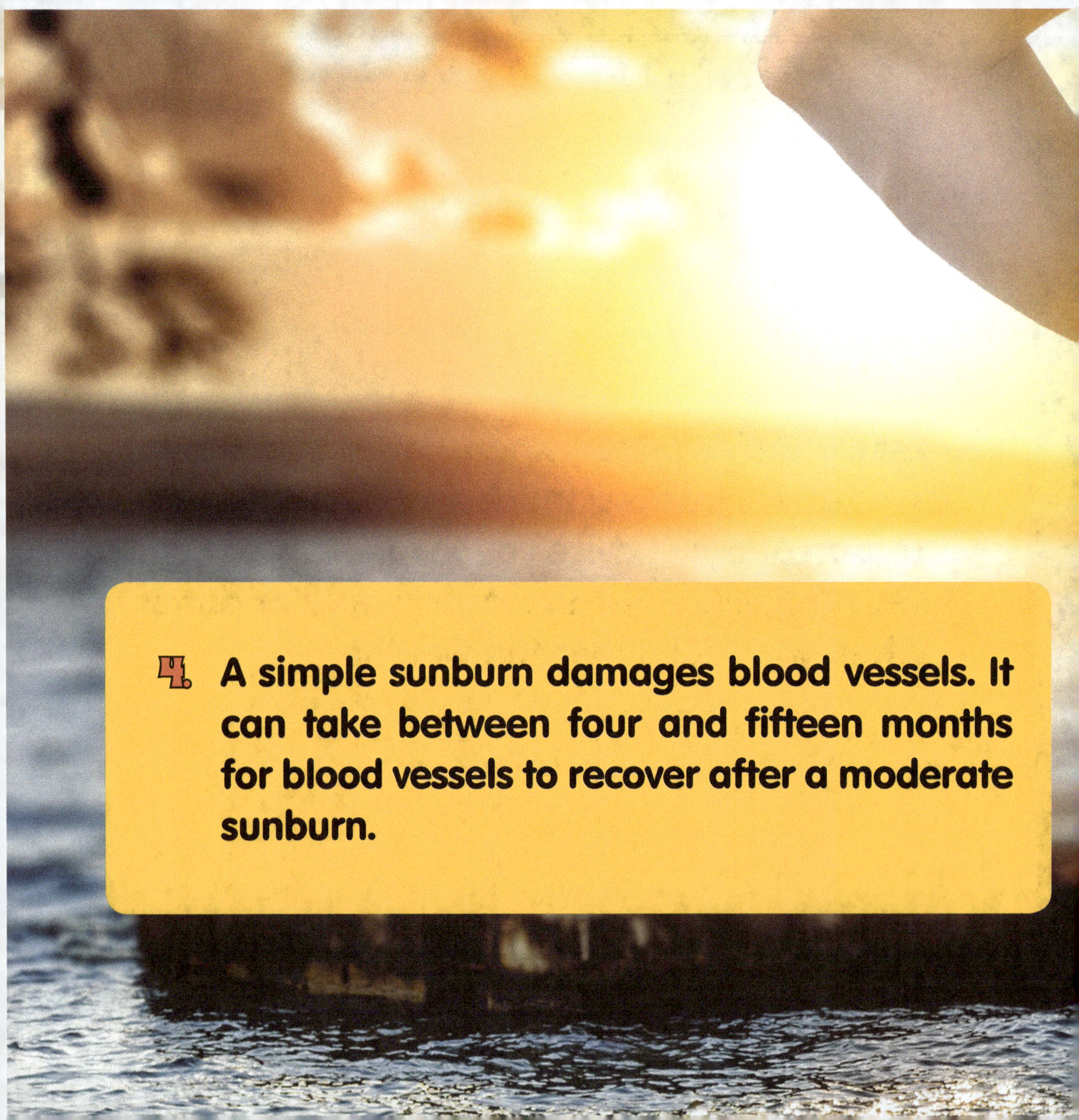
4. A simple sunburn damages blood vessels. It can take between four and fifteen months for blood vessels to recover after a moderate sunburn.

YOURS TO TAKE CARE OF

Your body is with you for your whole life. And the better you take care of it, the longer that life may be. Eat well, exercise regularly, and get lots of sleep... and keep your brain active by reading and learning from Baby Professor books!

Visit

BABY PROFESSOR
EDUCATION KIDS

www.BabyProfessorBooks.com

to download Free Baby Professor eBooks
and view our catalog of new and exciting
Children's Books